A

LOVE

AFFAIR

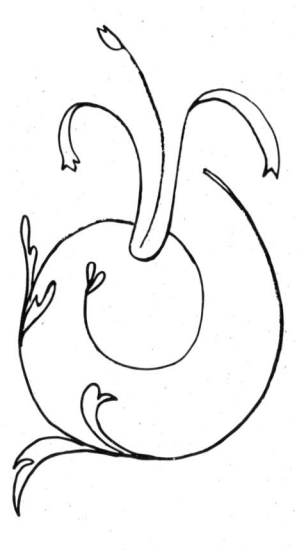

9
EDITOR'S NOTE

11
BLUE, BLUE, BRILLIANT BLUE
Carolina Ramirez-Figueroa

15
(FRAILEJÓN)
Mónica Rivas Velásquez

20
SUPERCRITICAL, A PSALM
Adam Moore

23
BEING A LOVER OF WINE
Andrea Cetrulo

26
THE PARIS FOLLIES
Himali Singh Soin

44
MARSEILLE CANAL
John Bingham-Hall

47
**LUNAR CAUSTIC:
A MEMORY WITHIN A GRAIN OF SALT**
Marta Michalowska

56
DUA NE GYABIDIE
Labeja Kodua Okullu

61
HOMES(EA)CK
Fani Kostourou

67
THE VIEW
Theo Turpin

71
COLLECTIVE DISPLAY OF AFFECTION
Lea Collet, Miriam Austin, Harry Bix, Guendalina Cerruti,
Rosa Doornenbal, Roxman Gatt, Maria Gorodeckaya,
Natalia Januła, Eleni Papazoglou, Anna Souter, Zaiba Jabbar,
Lou-Atessa Marcellin, Naz Balkaya, Dylan Spencer-Davidson

77
NOTES ON LETTERS

85
BIOGRAPHIES

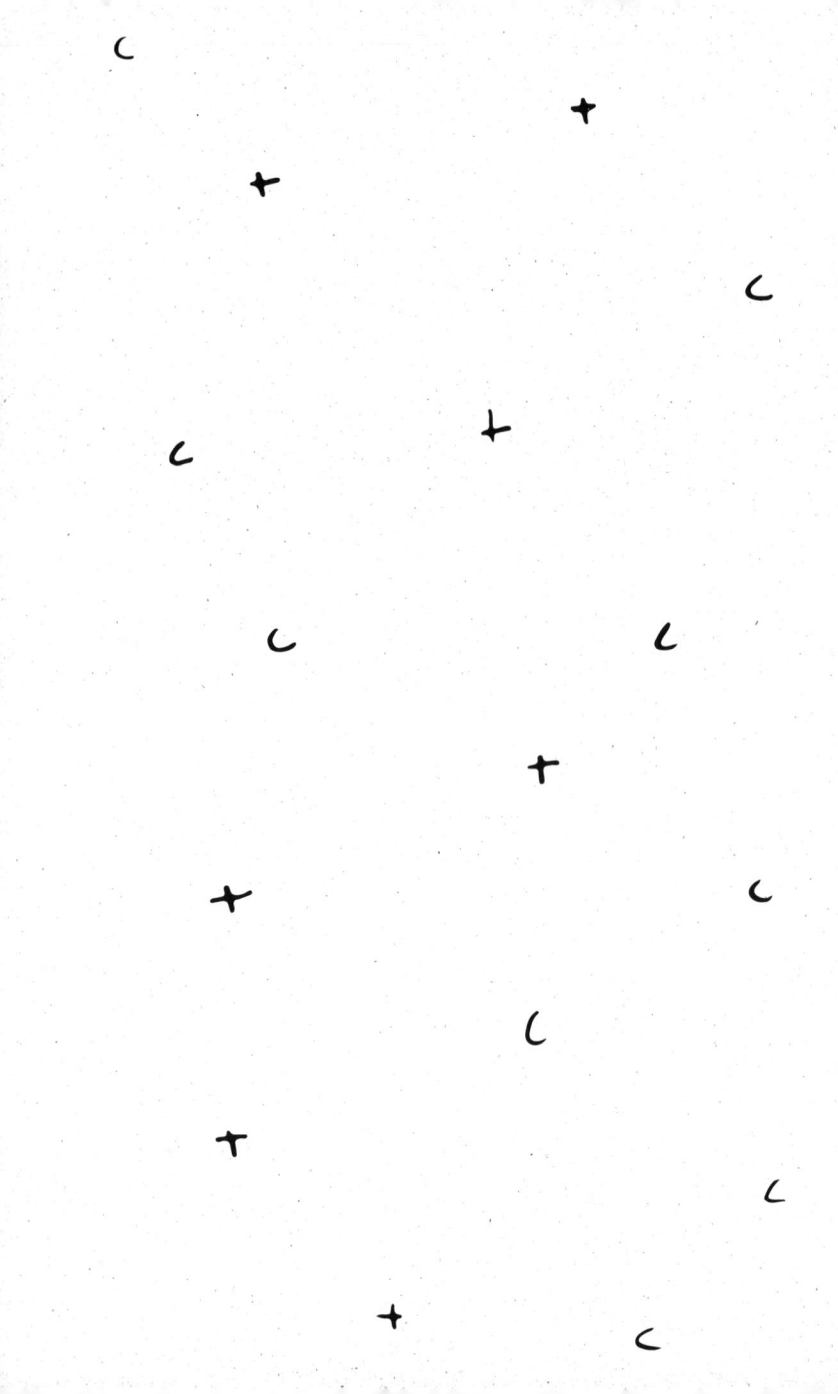

This is Love.
All strings attached.
Emotions
Joy
Despair

Collectively felt
Collectively lived
Collectively remembered.

A *Love Affair* is a collection of twelve love letters addressed to the human and the more-than-human. The letters speak of the ineffable, they speak of 'transformative encounters',[1] of contamination, and being in love. They embark on an intimate journey of collected fragments, of time capsules and of (im)possible love. Contributors become bodies of water, crumbs on tables, follies to take refuge in. These letters attempt to connect with personal and collective memories through affect rather than logic, allowing ourselves to feel and to move together in and out of love.

Seeing through my eyelids, shades of red, jaunting with the cosmos without burning. I can feel the sun dripping along my body, unable to breath, the pores of my skin are crying. The cat is licking my hand, grating dead cells; to them I'm a salty entremet, them and I in osmosis. I've become a textured coffee bean, ground in the early morning for the pleasure of campers. Lying down, looking up, they put the remains of my body on their black skin. Skin to skin, we fuse, we merge, we mutate, my cells with their DNA. They wash me out with a tie- dye tshirt, and later will dip me into the river. Transformed again. I feel like I'm a membrane, holding others, being extended by their presence seeping through me. To be contaminated is a beautiful thing but to be poisoned can be fatal. I can only hold so many of you.

This book is interested in feeling(s) as a source of knowledge(s) and placing care and affection as paramount to creating what we could term, through a reading of American anthropologist Anna Tsing, assemblages for collaborative survival. The letters present tools for uncovering what those assemblages can look and feel like and how we can attune ourselves to others to create new worlds.

—Lou-Atessa Marcellin

1   Anna Tsing, *The Mushroom at the end of the World*

BLUE, BLUE, BRILLIANT BLUE

CAROLINA RAMIREZ-FIGUEROA

I was young when I found you, *Paenibacillus*,
Scared and inexperienced,
Uncertain was my every day.

Tel Aviv is a long way.
So many safety rules,
Formal protocols to meet.
I was nervous, didn't know what to expect

I'll say it without shame—I wanted to control you

They warned me to keep you happy,
So you would follow my desires,
Take the form of my imagination,
Dynamically adapt,
Just for me

(Steps to follow,
Meeting in-between worlds)

Everyone had an opinion.
They say you're intelligent,
Call you simple and easy;
Others say you're disposable, contingent.

I met an artist in Japan who prayed for you,
An altar for the sacrifice of your kin.
We shall worship them and we shall war them

You were always difficult to find,
You're ethereal, fashioned out of air.
Translucent, a shapeshifter of sorts.

There are ways of finding you,
You stain in blue,
Blue, blue, brilliant blue

We speak in movements,
choreographies and dance,
My hands still remember
(In my dreams I wave and sweep).

If I kept you content, you would duplicate,
Pattern beautifully for me.
Your flagella twist and turn,
What a wondrous swirl

Your mixed signals, my anger bubbles up.
Are you my companion? My partner in crime?
An intruder? Friend or foe?
Are you here to hurt me? Be a pathogen in my life?

At night my mind craves you

There are so many things that separate us
Each day it's harder to find you.
I've lost you,
and I don't know where to find me

You introduced me to chaos,
And I yearn for the days we spent together,
For the rhythms,
And the way my body learned yours,

I've learned to care for you,
to fear you,
I depend on you as you on me.
Can we acknowledge each other?

(FRAILEJÓN)

MÓNICA RIVAS VELÁSQUEZ

(frailejón)

                                                        Of the
                                                        day,
                                                   I have 25

                                                 photographs.

I   Páramo
  write
    to you   high altitude forests
      diagonally,   OF
      through
        memories.   tropical
                                        Andes AND
      Before
        stepping in, we   contrast of
          take two steps   scorching sun IS
        back

                                        BY freezing nights
              1995—family road   highly efficient
              trip, near el Valle   AT capturing
                del Cocora, passing quantities of
                  through el páramo, water from
                    spotting   fogs and
                      frailejones   rains,
                  while heading
                  towards
                    el Nevado del
                      Ruiz for a
                        short
                              walk.

THEN
rich peat
soils
Release
into streams
thin silvery
hairs
reflecting light
and absorbing   (infection)
water

                           it is this
I think of you—   mountain,
mediation: through the
how some   window,
encounters   the moving
happen mostly   window, in my
from the car,   memory—
through the   part of what
window and   I am concerned
the camera.   about:

A persisting   the
memory that   the landscapes that   ground
becomes a   keep returning   covered
different   to voice themselves   by grass
type of   all the voices they   a sanctuary
thought   hold   a goddess
                                                            memories
               el pliegue de   a mine
               la montaña
               la cordillera
               the soil

Meditation as in-betweenness

We
came
across
the
páramo
almost by
chance,
visiting el
Valle del Cocora.
I don't remember
much more from
the trip.

It was mostly being
on the road, turning
round, and the land
showing, appearing
suddenly.

La distancia
(remoteness)
el entretejido

Can your
leaves bounce
back somehow
to the London
ones—
the ones I
went chasing
that year
on
lockdown
walks

El Cocora, los musgos,
las montañas grises
y rosadas
antes del Ruiz,
pero sobretodo,
los frailejones
y el
páramo.

a coming
together

Do we
turn into
you, for
instance,
every time
we pour water?

Is mirroring a way
of listening?

How is this/that different from learning?

that measure your distance to the rainforest through travelling water in the shape of clouds, can they be a way to touch you if I go walking in the fog?

And the main in-between

los rios voladores / the flying rivers

https://vimeo.com/569087570

SUPERCRITICAL, A PSALM

```
        M M
     A
              O

   D
                R
 A

                  E
```

My soles glide
On Faith I ride
Every revolution is a paddle to the tide
Oceanic breathing every beat is a vibe
Charging sunken haem beneath my lipid container
With those pools up above and these pools in my eyes
Supercritical, every breath is a dive
Colourful, I reflect the skies
Outside I shine
At my shores I am sure

Coursing like beads on the film on the froth
On the foam I roam aloft

My currents shiver, and blades of light quiver, diaphanous gravities
                                                ripple through soft

Queering, as distant moons reach in my mare
Mare Humorum, Mare Imbrium, Mare Insularum, Mare Nubium,
the moisture, the showers and rains on my islands,
                             the clouds in the sky, all are water, are I
Hot springs and vapours, tempests and blizzards
Dark of my slippages—down in the depths—
the static shallows of my heart's warp and weft
are rushing and rushing
and splashing and gushing
My palatial glacial straits
At my shores I roar

Sharp corners round into bends when I roll
Rivers rolling out to sea, rivers stilled within me
Inside I'm wide

At my shores I endure

Every inhalation is a promise I keep
Every exhalation is a vow I repeat
Every dip I take is an oath I speak

I shimmer
I roar
My palatial glacial straits
are wide
I am tidal
At my shores I am sure

https://vimeo.com/644819461

BEING A LOVER OF WINE

ANDREA

CERTULO

Love disrupts social hierarchies and
transcends logic and language. So does
good wine. It demands our tasting
tongue to silence the speaking one, to
embrace the given, that which comes to
us without asking. Ecstatic love. Love
of the world. Love that ferments *with*
time. Spiritual ecstasy that precedes
and transcends language. Like love,
good wine is anarchic: an antidote
to the perpetuation of conventional
order, it is chaotic, entropic—it resists
elegantly, silently. Grace. Grape. Good

wine refutes standardisation through its singularity: no single bottle
resembles another; it cannot be encapsulated in a monolithic, all
encompassing label. Wine negates a social order where consumption
is often mistaken for truly experiencing the world. The master is not
whose hand swirls the glass and whose mouth judges gratuitously.
It is the producer, the soiled, the alchemist, the sapient drinker, the
true lover of wine. In the hands of the wrong producer or consumer,
wine may even become a poisonous substance (an anodyne
experience, a bad hangover, anaesthetized drunkenness...).

§

All knowledge passes through the senses

What is to be defined as *good wine*, and more importantly, do we
need a definition? For that matter, what is good taste anyway; who is
to judge? What if one were to accept that, like good wine, good taste
is simply ineffable? To accept this is to accept taking the winding,
unknown path that leads to discernment rather than the straight,

speedy highway towards rationality and stratification of the world. To define sapience, the Sufis (who themselves invented good taste) opted for the Arabic term *Dhawk*, a term that denotes the arduous task of unveiling and accessing the divine through direct experience and intuition. Wine, a symbol of the divine, cannot be understood cerebrally but must be tasted and experienced. When we drink wine we engage in a temporarily sensuous act, and it is in the midst of this temporality that we rise to a higher plane, becoming convinced that the divine can be accessed on earth.

§

Cosmos and prima materia

One of the early Greek alchemical texts places Sagittarius as the astrological sign of fermentation. Lunar phases and zodiac signs guide the hands of the master alchemist, the winemaker: from liquid to solid, from solid to liquid, dissolving and bridging the material with the spiritual world. Alchemy transforms the elements. Winemaking is alchemy. It is natural mysticism. It seeks to transform the given without violating its natural structure. In descending yet not hierarchical order (the generosity of wine does not allow for such rigid arrangements): the alchemy of wine commences from the firmament, down to rain, dew, air, salt, earth, and back to the celestial realm, carried in the bodies and spirits of ecstatic wine drinkers. A recurring cycle. Through winemaking, the terroir (or earth) becomes fluid geology. Animal secretions, sex, dust, rain, fungi, manure, straw, bacteria... each bottle is infused with the singularity of its terroir. 'What/where am I tasting?' My speaking tongue wants to describe again! Unclean, unfiltered, unpasteurized.

§

THE PARIS FOLLIES

HIMALI SINGH SOIN

No theme requires more pure logic than love.
        —Alain Badiou, *What is Love.*

On this day, the 1st of April, a fool's day,
I post my first note from Paris, city of beautiful
foolishness. Paris, La Ville Lumière, meaning
city of light, meaning photons travelling at us
at a finite speed, meaning what we see in the
present is already in the not-so-distant past.
Named in light of its boulevards of gas lamps and
its role in the Enlightenment, the Paris of science
and reason coexists with its Romantic inclinations. Its architectural
symmetries are varied, from functional to completely frivolous.
The city of light and the city of love are created for each other.
The Paris of Voltaire is also the Paris of Proust.

    Architectural follies are visual structures that serve no purpose
beyond ornamentation. They are created for sheer delight, madness,
displacement.

    In sport, when the score is zero, we say 'love,' because love is
for nothing, love itself is a folly. In his chapter on the love letter in *A Lover's Discourse*, Barthes differentiates between a correspondence
and a letter. A correspondence, mathematically, is one in which the
writer tries to make a point, to have a function. But, he says, 'for the
lover, the letter has no tactical value: it is purely expressive—at most,
flattering (but here flattery is not a matter of self-interest, merely the
language of devotion); what I engage in with the other is a relation,
not a correspondence: the relation brings together two images. You
are everywhere, your image is total, in various ways.'[1]

    I will follow architectural follies and address their particular
desires in a trail of twelve love letters, one for each hour of the clock.
I will Google translate these letters, so that they jumble in the
possibly chance-like, algorithmic chaos of love itself, and will post

them here. But before that, they will be left at a site of another folly: on street corners; on park benches and beneath doors; for strangers to chance upon, read, throw out or use to make wild declarations of their feelings. I will use a carbonless lab notebook that makes copies of these letters as I write them, dismissing the uniqueness of the letter, the distinction of love, relegating it to any other passer-by's extravagance, an indulgence, a folly. I will not wait for an answer.

The tone of the letters will straddle this very line between it and me, reason and un-reason, between knowing and not-knowing, grasping at this city full of light even as the light grasps at us. The reason behind every reason might be to be, finally, without reason.

1 April 2015

Dear Folly No. 1,

We never really began, did we? We haven't ended yet. But that is the way anything is—you of all people know that time is not linear, that the past may be equal to, or run simultaneously with, the future. Archimedes knew this too. Perhaps it is because the earth is round that we designed our clocks this way too, I don't know. I like to think that I am a newel—sans recurrence and always the same—and you wrap around me, twisted, entangled, spinning about my axis, never moving—and always so—forward or back. Gravity gives me weight but I long for the lift, while you lust after the earth. Sometimes I think perhaps you are in love with the soil or the sky, and I am a mere medium. Lost or lonely, you spiral toward neither and nor, repeating and reusing your lyrics, over and over. Your symmetry is helical. The more I exist, the further you forget; the less I wait, the greater the weight. I make right angles in your radius, I navigate your night, but you have already fled into the new light.

$\Delta, |\text{-}|.$

1 Avril 2015

Cher Folly n° 1,

Nous ne avons jamais vraiment commencé que nous avons fait; nous ne avons pas encore terminé. Mais ce est la façon dont tout est-vous de toutes les personnes savent que le temps ne est pas linéaire, que le passé peut être égal, ou fonctionner simultanément avec, l'avenir. Archimède savait trop. Peut-être ce est que la terre est ronde que nous avons conçu nos horloges de cette façon aussi, je ne sais pas. Je aime à penser que je suis que newel-sans récidive et toujours le même et vous enroulez autour de moi, tordu, empêtré, la filature de mon axe, jamais en mouvement et toujours si-avant ou en arrière. Gravity me donne du poids, mais je ai longtemps pour l'ascenseur, vous convoiter la terre. Parfois, je pense que peut-être vous êtes en amour avec le sol ou le ciel, et je suis un simple moyen. Perdu ou solitaire, vous spirale vers ni et ni, en répétant et en réutilisant vos paroles, encore et encore. Votre symétrie est helical. Le plus que je existe, plus vous oublier, moins je, attends plus le poids. Je fais angle droit dans votre rayon, je navigue votre soirée, mais vous avez déjà fui dans la nouvelle lumière.

Δ, |-|.

2 April 2015

Dear Folly No. 2,

I know you sometimes better than you know you and sometimes not at all and sometimes both at the same time. But this is not about knowledge.

    There are thresholds everywhere. Membranes of coincidence, seepage, simultaneity and resistance. Fences, made of steel or milkweed, between daydream and reverie, hypothesis and wish-fulfilment, the naive and the dishonest, line consciousness. You did not keep your word.

Δ, |-|.

2 Avril 2015

Cher Folly n° 2,

~~Je vous connais parfois mieux que vous vous connaissez et parfois pas du tout et parfois les deux en même temps. Mais ce ne est pas sur la connaissance.~~

Il y'a des seuils partout. Membranes de coïncidence, l'infiltration, la simultanéité et la résistance. Clôtures, en acier ou en asclépias, entre rêverie et à la rêverie, les hypothèses et accomplissement de désir, le naïf et la conscience de ligne malhonnête. Vous ne avez pas tenu votre parole.

Δ, |-|.

3 April 2015

Dear Folly No. 3,

You absorb the world even as you reflect it back. You are not alone but you do not have the privilege of the private either. You are made of fairy tales and fables but you contain neither images of rural landscapes nor portraits of pretty girls sitting for a painter, who see their beauty for the first time, nor mirrors, glass or metal. You are made up of only the wall and yet how can a wall ever be only a wall? You are made of water.

You are beautiful. I can't say that enough. In a classical kind of way, in silence, in thought that is not distant or indifferent, but immediate. In music. You are autumn and spring simultaneously. You are the windows, the moss, the tree, me. You are a true rebel. You resurrect the earth by calling out to it. You are the aristocracy without airs, the working bourgeois, the queen and her subjects. You are non-confrontational. And that is why you do not function, you are not complicit.

Δ, |-|.

3 Avril 2015

Cher Folly n° 3,

Vous absorbez le monde alors même que vous la renvoient. Vous n'êtes pas seul, mais vous ne avez pas le privilège du privé soit. Vous êtes fait de contes de fées et des fables mais vous ne contiennent ni images de paysages ou portraits de jolies filles assises pour un peintre qui voit sa beauté pour la première fois, ni miroirs, verre ou en métal rurales. Vous êtes constitué de seulement le mur et encore comment un mur peut jamais être seulement un mur? Vous êtes fait de l'eau. Tu est magnifique. Je ne peux pas dire que suffisant. Dans un genre classique de la façon dont, dans le silence, dans la pensée qui ne est pas lointain ou indifférent, mais immédiate. Dans la musique.

    Vous êtes automne et au printemps simultanément. Vous êtes les fenêtres, la mousse, l'arbre, moi. Vous êtes un vrai rebelle. Vous ressuscitez la terre en appelant à elle. Vous êtes l'aristocratie sans airs, les bourgeois de travail, la reine et ses sujets. Vous êtes non conflictuelle. Et ce est pourquoi vous ne fonctionnent pas, vous n'êtes pas complices.

$\Delta, |\text{-}|.$

4 April 2015

Dear Folly No. 4,

Your structure is about feeling, but made without feeling. Held up by fragile, tentacular columns of sand eroded by water, uninviting even to termites, your own stanchions are resilient. The circumference of your dome is equal to its centre. Your velocity, the only invariant with which you coexist, is orthogonal to your centripetal force. I circuit around your middle, verge of your radius, lipline round rim, at the brink of circumspection, helm of every horizon. I cannot really enter even after I have entered. My only ablution here is air. You are solitary but without self. This was not my neoclassical fantasy.

I mean, you're beautiful. I can't say that enough. In a purposefully timeless kind of way, like music. Like if Kate Bush sang about the protomodernist novel inside you. In an orange bubble, vocal chords lost in some monolithic echo of soprano and suppressed silence.

Your love also runs orthogonal to your tempo. Some might believe it's eternal, but I know that is not so.

$\Delta, |\text{-}|.$

4 Avril 2015

Cher Folly n° 4,

Votre structure est à propos de sentiment, mais faite sans sentiment. Tenu par fragiles, colonnes tentaculaires de sable érodé par l'eau, peu attirante, même aux termites, vos propres chandeliers sont élastique. La circonférence de votre dôme est égal à son centre. Votre vitesse, le seul invariant avec lequel vous coexistent, est orthogonale à votre force centripète. Je circuit autour de votre milieu, point de votre rayon, la ligne de lèvre rim rond, au bord de la circonspection, tête de tous les horizons. Je ne peux pas vraiment entrer même après que je suis entré. Mon seul ablutions ici est l'air. Vous êtes solitaire, mais sans auto. Ce ne était pas mon fantasme néoclassique.

Je veux dire, tu es belle. Je ne peux pas dire que suffisant. Dans une sorte délibérément intemporelle de passage, dans la musique. Comme si Kate Bush chanson sur proto roman moderniste intérieur de vous. Dans une bulle d'orange, cordes vocales perdus dans quelque écho monolithique de soprano et supprimées silence.

Votre amour gère également orthogonale à votre tempo. Certains pourraient croire que ce est éternel, mais je sais que ce ne est pas ainsi.

$\Delta, |\text{-}|.$

5 April 2015

Dear Folly No. 5,

Perhaps it is because the earth is round that we designed our clocks this way too, I don't know. There's something about making a grid in a circle that is comforting; it is as though you can be a point on a line and still view the whole line, but the circle is always curving away, no matter how I hang the clock. 12 o'clock north, 3 o'clock north, the second hand, then the minute, the hour, keeps on ticking onward. Not forward necessarily—sometimes I imagine turning all the clocks everywhere back. Would time repeat itself? Or does it work the other way around: is it because our clocks move in the same pattern over and over that we form habit? Anyway, here, where we are, the clocks don't work. You are always eternally young and infinitely old, you are not the seasons, the shadow, the water. You do not tell time. You drink rosé in the morning and prove theorems in colour and boil eggs for centuries and think satellites are real stars and believe me when I say nature made language. The continents are still drifting apart, but with you I no longer live four hours ahead. I live in time without time, without dates or distances. Time, when stopped, broken, becomes continuous, without beginning or end, like a rock or the whole sky.

    This is an indefinite interval.

$\Delta, |-|.$

5 Avril 2015

Cher Folly n° 5,

Peut-être ce est que la terre est ronde que nous avons conçu nos horloges de cette façon aussi, je ne sais pas. Il ya quelque chose en faisant une grille dans un cercle qui est réconfortant, comme vous pouvez être un point sur une ligne et voir encore toute la ligne, mais le cercle est toujours courbant loin, peu importe comment je accroche l'horloge, 12 heures au nord, 3 heures au nord, l'aiguille des

secondes, puis les minutes, l'heure, avance à grands pas en avant.
Pas nécessairement en avant:
   parfois je imagine tourner toutes les horloges partout dos;
sera le temps se répète? Ou ça marche dans l'autre sens, parce que
nos horloges se déplacent dans le même schéma encore et que
nous formons habitude? Quoi qu'il en soit, ici, où nous sommes,
les horloges ne fonctionnent pas. Vous êtes toujours éternellement
jeune et infiniment vieux, vous n'êtes pas les saisons, l'ombre, l'eau.
Vous ne dites pas le temps. Vous buvez rosé le matin et prouver
des théorèmes de couleur et faites bouillir les oeufs pendant des
siècles et que les satellites sont de véritables étoiles et croyez-moi
quand je dis Nature fait la langue. Les continents sont toujours
à la dérive en dehors, mais avec vous, je ne vivent plus quatre
heures d'avance. Je habite dans le temps sans temps, sans dates
ou des distances. Temps, à l'arrêt, cassé, devient continu, sans
commencement ni fin, comme un rocher ou tout le ciel. Ce est un
intervalle indéterminée.

$$\Delta, |\text{-}|.$$

17 APRIL 2015

Dear Folly No. 6,
That which is round is not necessarily whole.

$$\Delta, |\text{-}|.$$

17 AVRIL 2015

Cher Folly n° 6,
Ce qui est ronde ne est pas nécessairement ensemble.

$$\Delta, |\text{-}|.$$

18 April 2015

Dear Folly No. 7,

What happened here? What epics were performed, how many villains killed in your amphitheatre? Your half-eaten pillars flicker in the stagnant reflection of the algae-veneered pond that lies in the wake of your history.

 The pigeons settle into your moss because they know the moss has an instinct for the magnificent. I have found terrible beauty in ruin, but there is nothing chic about you. You make me melancholic, knowing that the stories of before will be lost later—and in their wake, pieces like you—circular repetition half undone standing up supporting nothing for no purpose or present.

 This is our eternal condition—searching for a static moment in time.

Δ, |-|.

18 Avril 2015

Cher Folly n° 7,

Qu'est-il arrivé ici? Que épopées ont été effectuées, combien méchants tué dans votre amphithéâtre? Vos piliers de moitié mangé scintillent dans la réflexion stagnante de l'étang d'algues-plaqué qui se trouve dans le sillage de votre histoire.

 Les pigeons se installent dans votre mousse parce qu'ils savent la mousse a un instinct pour le magnifique.

 Je ai trouvé terrible beauté en ruine, mais il n'y a rien chic, sur vous. Vous me faites mélancolique sachant que les histoires de devant seront perdus plus tard et dans leur sillage, des morceaux comme vous, la répétition circulaire moitié Undone debout soutenant rien pour aucun but ou présente.

 Ce est notre condition éternelle – la recherche d'un moment statique dans le temps.

Δ, |-|.

19 April 2015

Dear Folly No. 8,

You used to ring in noon, then the same sun that you channelled, magnifying heat, burned you. After dark, the libertines wove complex polyamorous webs of sex and play and drank wine and read Euripides out loud, all administered by your private government. Your five metals—iron, copper, gold, bronze, lead—attest to this secularism. Now you have no time, no direction. In this, your spiralling intuition is perhaps more sensitive to the way we really work: the world is laced with labyrinths. Borges will attest to this, as will our natural scientists. We walk inward only to find ourselves walking outward. You are older than Paris, older than the Eiffel tower, as old as light almost. And yet, if I moved around you in the opposite direction, you would be paradoxically young, younger than your previous self. It's like your ghosts and your afterlives live simultaneously, in a swirl, but with difference. In this enantiodromia of shadow and self is some harmonious imbalance of infinite kindness without imposed morality. In fact, your aesthetic is political: in this labyrinth that winds around a smug illusion of choice, your fatalism is free of finality.

Δ, |-|.

19 Avril 2015

Cher Folly n° 8,

Vous avez utilisé pour sonner le midi, puis le même soleil que vous canalisé, grossissant la chaleur, vous brûlé. À la nuit tombée, les libertins tissaient toiles polyamoureux complexes du sexe et de jouer et buvaient du vin et de lire à haute voix Euripide, tous administrés par votre gouvernement privé.

Votre cinq métaux—fer, cuivre, or, bronze, plomb—témoignent de cette laïcité. Maintenant, vous ne avez pas le temps, pas de direction. En cela, votre intuition spirale est peut-être plus sensibles à la façon dont nous travaillons vraiment: le monde est truffé de labyrinthes.

Borges se en témoigner, de même que nos spécialistes des sciences naturelles. Nous marchons vers l'intérieur que de nous trouver en marchant vers l'extérieur. Vous êtes âgé de Paris, plus que la tour Eiffel, aussi vieux que la lumière presque. Et pourtant, si je ai déménagé autour de vous dans la direction opposée, vous êtes jeune, paradoxalement, plus jeune que votre auto précédente. Ce est comme vos fantômes et vos vies posthumes vivent simultanément, dans un tourbillon, mais avec la différence. Dans ce énantiodromie d'ombre et de soi-même est un certain déséquilibre harmonieux de la bonté infinie sans moralité imposée. En fait, votre esthétique est politique: dans ce labyrinthe qui serpente autour d'une illusion béate de choix, votre fatalisme est libre de finalité.

Δ, |-|.

20 April 2015

Dear Folly No. 9,
Your body is pixelated.

Δ, |-|.

20 Avril 2015

Cher Folly n° 9,
Votre corps est pixélisé.

Δ, |-|.

21 April 2015

Dear Folly No. 10,
You are not a folly. You are speculative, irrational, idolatry, anthropomorphic, funny. You're the guy at the bar who begins, 'what did zero say to infinity?' You read everything backwards, upside down.

    Your mom is wow. You were a caesarean. You do not like paragraphs.

You like:
1. Ladders
2. Plastic shower curtains
3. Red light bulbs
4. Skinny black jeans
5. Signing your name with your initial
6. Balloons
7. Reading about the sky
8. Listening to things that can't be heard
9. Pale ale
10. Children, trollies full
11. Only one kind of girl:
a. Petite
b. Books. She's read them all
c. She likes math
d. She likes hip hop
e. She likes streams
f. She doesn't like papaya
g. She likes orange
h. She gets H
i. She likes metaphor jokes
j. She is far away
k. She lets you hold the door for her:
I. Only when you're at a bar
II. When you've answered the riddle
III. The answer is 'nice belt'
IV. You've laughed
V. You want to say nothing and kiss
VI. You wait
VII. You don't kiss. You go home and lie awake till you have to get up again.

Δ, |-|.

21 Avril 2015

Cher Folly n° 10,

Vous n'êtes pas une folie. Vous êtes spéculative, irrationnel, l'idolâtrie, anthropomorphe, drôle. Vous êtes le gars au bar qui commence, 'qu'est-ce que dire de zéro à l'infini?'. Vous avez lu tout à l'envers, la tête en bas. Votre maman est wow. Vous étiez une césarienne. Vous ne aimez pas les paragraphes.

    Tu aimes:

        1. Échelles

        2. Rideaux de douche en plastique

        3. Ampoules rouges

        4. Jean noir skinny

        5. Signature de votre nom avec votre initiale

        6. Ballons

        7. Lire sur le ciel

        8. Écoute de choses qui ne peuvent être entendues

        9. Ale pale

        10. Enfants, les chariots pleins

        11. Un seul genre de fille:

        a. Petite

        b. Livres. Elle les lire tous

        c. Elle aime les mathématiques

        d. Elle aime le hip hop

        e. Elle aime flux si

        f. Elle ne aime pas la papaye

        g. Elle aime h orange

        h. Elle obtient H

        i. Elle aime les blagues de métaphore

        j. Elle est loin

        k. Elle nous allons vous détenez la porte pour elle:

        I. Seulement quand vous êtes dans un bar

        II. Lorsque vous avez répondu à l'énigme

III. La réponse est «belle ceinture»
   IV. Vous avez ri
   V. Vous voulez rien et baiser dire.
   VI. Vous attendez
   VII. Vous ne embrasse pas. Vous rentrez chez vous et
       rester éveillé jusqu'à ce que vous avez à se relever.
                    Δ, |-|.

                                                    22 April 2015
Dear Folly No. 11,
Someone asked me if I'd written to you about infidelity yet. Page 18 fell out, I haven't written to anybody else. But if it's because the world is comprised of fractals that we see patterns everywhere, then of course we cannot love only one once.

    I suppose I haven't written about infidelity because I dont quite believe in it—love triangles have existed since the beginning of time and you—the epic tower of Eiffel—ancient Egypt—are testament to this. Even modernity hasn't altered the shape in which we write stories. Besides, the world of capital is comprised of pyramids: giant triangles made up of triangles, steel and built to absorb every shock. It is the world without argument, the break in the dialectic, the third man apotheosis postulated by the man of pyramids himself—Aristotle.

    But this break in duality also means an infinite recurrence of the 'third,' a world in which two entities do not exist outside a third space—thought—that activates them. In our identical, reproductive, egocentric view of the three, the triangle is both a symbol of positivism and balance.

    I have been with somebody else, I won't apologize for that. It has built a tension in me—some nonlinear integral equation with the ability to channel all counter-balancing wind forces (I stole that from wikipedia). You trust me less, I suspect, (because of wikipedia or because of the cheating?) but here I am, bound by your lattice, promising that the third man we should really worry about is the distance.

That taut area between military desire and humanitarianism, between the 19th century and the 21st, between your music and mine. How the air passed through your wrought iron arms, how you stand infinitely light and solid, lurid in repetition, beating on and on, with the same measure, knowing better than all of us that it is not a matter of time, but space. Also, your throat looked beautiful in the postcard with your photograph on it. You looked far away though, like a cliché.

Δ, |-|.

22 Avril 2015

Cher Folly n° 11,
Quelqu'un m'a demandé si je avais encore écrit de vous sur l'infidélité. Page 18 est tombé, je ne ai pas écrit à personne d'autre. Mais si ce est parce que le monde est composé de fractales que nous voyons partout des motifs, alors bien sûr nous ne pouvons pas aimer une seule fois avec un.

Je suppose que je nai pas écrit au sujet de l'infidélité parce que je ne crois assez en elle-triangles amoureux ont existé depuis le début des temps et vous-la tour Eiffel-épique de l'Egypte ancienneté moignent de cela. Même la modernité n'a pas modifié la forme dans laquelle nous écrivons des histoires.

En outre, le monde du capital est composé de pyramides: triangles géants constitués de triangles, de l'acier et construits pour absorber tous les chocs. Ce est le monde sans argument, la rupture dans la dialectique, le troisième homme apothéose postulé par l'homme lui-même de pyramides – Aristotle.

Mais cette rupture dans la dualité, ce est aussi une récurrence infinie de la «troisième», un monde dans lequel deux entités ne existent pas en dehors de la troisième pensé que les active. Dans notre vue identique, la reproduction, égocentrique des trois, le triangle est à la fois un symbole de positivisme et de l'équilibre.

Je ai été avec quelqu'un d'autre, je ne vais pas me en excuse. Il a construit une tension en moi - une certaine équation intégrale non-linéaire avec la capacité de canaliser toutes les forces du vent de contre-équilibrage, je ai volé que de wikipedia. Tu me fais confiance moins, je le soupçonne, (en raison de wikipedia ou en raison de la triche?), Mais je suis ici, lié par votre réseau, promettant que le troisième homme que nous devrions vraiment inquiéter est la distance. Cette zone tendue entre le désir militaire et humanitaire, entre le 19e siècle et le 21e, entre votre musique et la mienne.

Comment l'air traversé vos bras fer forgé, la façon dont vous vous tenez infiniment léger et solide, sinistre dans la répétition, battant ainsi de suite, avec la même mesure, connaissant mieux que nous tous que ce ne est pas une question de temps, mais l'espace. En outre, votre gorge était belle dans la carte postale avec votre photo sur elle. Vous avez cherché bien loin, comme un cliché.

Δ, |-|.

23 April 2015

Dear Folly No. 12,

Today marks one dozen letters to you. I suppose it does not matter if you do not respond, as long as you're feeling the feels. Here I am, at the door of modernity, waiting. It feels like everything has passed. It feels like all that's left are names, Mars, the great god of war. It feels like there is no one here, there is only waiting. And memories of poems, and numbers in no particular order, and street signs dented and pointing in obscure directions. It really matters, how we are, how far we can carry love, now, when the apocalypse is not only a stereotype, a tourist destination, it is one in which matter is of the utmost importance—a container, if broken—releasing the spirit of separation, flailing energy, everywhere.

Δ, |-|.

23 Avril 2015

Cher Folly n° 12,

Aujourd'hui marque une douzaine de lettres de vous. Je suppose que ce ne est pas grave si vous ne répondez pas, aussi longtemps que vous vous sentez les ressent.

Ici, je suis, à la porte de la modernité, en attendant. Il se sent comme tout a passé. Il se sent comme tout ce qui reste sont des noms, Mars, le grand dieu de la guerre.

Il se sent comme il n'y a personne ici, il ne attend. Et les souvenirs de poèmes, et des numéros sans ordre et de la rue des signes particuliers bosselés et pointant dans des directions obscures.

Ce qui compte vraiment, comment nous sommes, dans quelle mesure nous pouvons mener à l'amour, maintenant, quand l'apocalypse ne est pas seulement un stéréotype, une destination touristique, ce est celui dans lequel la matière est de l'importance— un récipient plus grand, libérant rompu si le esprit de séparation, agitant l'énergie, partout.

Δ, |-|.

1 Roland Barthes, *A Lover's Discourse: Fragments.*

MARSEILLE CANAL

JOHN BINGHAM HALL

Quel est l'étranger, derrière les barreaux?
Jugé comme un voleur d'eau.
—Christine and the Queens

Boulevard du Vallon 13015

Ticket machine indecipherable, train late. This is a city of friction, trajectories through it are as jagged as the mountaintops around it. Twisting, snaking, evasive, like the narrow walled streets I have to follow in order to trace your route. You never give yourself up easily, not like the other canals I know. A glimpse of a concrete aqueduct between houses, then you are lost again, as the street curves away to follow your contour around the hill, hidden to me down the slope.

Boulevard Lombard, 13015

To see you suddenly—placid, smooth, cool in this broken landscape of glass and metal. In the park where we last met, you were decorated—a brief moment of show. Otherwise, your bridges try not to reveal you, or perhaps you try not to be revealed by them. You keep your distance, skirting and looking down on the city you hydrate. From here, with you, it seems like an assault, that urbanity, when we're together amongst quiet houses on a cool hill, as *jardins ouvriers* drip down your flank.

Jardins du Castellas, 13015

I know I won't always remember to think of you when I switch on my tap or close my eyes under a cold shower in summer. But you'll be on my mind the day the restrictions come. Then they'll know your name. Will they love you for feeding them all these years, or hate you because it wasn't enough? Sometimes it seems as if you wish you were a mountain stream—innocent, without expectation.

Is that why they made you a weir, so you froth and babble white, keeping you content while you toil for us?

Canal de Marseille, 13014

As we meander together across the back of the city, there's no more street. I join your path, illicitly, but your broken fences and open gates let me know I'm not the first one to seek you out. In fact, I saw one of them. Taking your bank as if it was merely a shortcut rather than a precious, stolen ribbon. He pointedly ignored me—I don't know if it was out of indifference or shame. The shame of two thieves passing each other in the night, or the indifference of a city street transposed onto this quasi rural hillside.

Chemin du Four de Buze, 13014

I haven't seen you in a while. I've been getting to know the world around you. This world of closed *bastides* whose dogs warn me off, of retirement homes in the form of Provençal villages, but also of glimpses of realities that seem so at odds with the city. Shared gardens drinking from their proximity to you are like post-disaster utopias—they might be the last chance at survival for a lucky few once police once again guard the water, as they did before you were built.

Rue des Aygadiers, 13013

I have to leave you here. Despite your abundance, I can neither eat nor drink from you, until you have been transformed, segregated and squeezed through a thousand conduits, into the dense city below where I will find nourishment. But I'll follow you again, of that I'm sure.

https://tinyurl.com/c49fvm5c

LUNAR CAUSTIC: A MEMORY WITHIN A GRAIN OF SALT

MARTA MICHAŁOWSKA

AgNO$_3$

There are photographs that carry latent power within their thin, flat bodies.

> Argentous nitrate
> Silver mononitrate
> Silver nitrate

That force is akin to magic, transferred from their negative doubles under a faint red light.

> Nitric acid silver (I) salt
> Nitric acid silver (1+) salt

Their blacks are opaque, containing all that resides in shadows. Their whites make you squint, holding all that is too much to capture in an image.

> 231-853-9[1]

But it is the greys, the subtle tones, that arrest what had happened in front of the lens

> lapis infernalis

a 1/60th of a second

> lunar caustic

---

[1] European Community (EC) Number, European Chemicals Agency (ECHA)

more or less

    odourless
    colourless
    bitter

a trace / a relic / a speck / a crumb

    inorganic

remains of a moment

    antiseptic
    germicidal
    astringent
    caustic

*

My grandfather was a chemist and an enthusiast photographer. In 1944, he had taken a photograph I was to find decades later. The image had been tucked inbetween the pages of an album featuring photographs of my father as a baby and had never had a dedicated place within it marked by remnants of glue. There was no trace of adhesive on the back of the photograph either.

    The album ended up in my possession following my father's death in 2007. 'Maybe you can do something with these,' my mother said, handing me the collection of images recording the earliest moments of my father's life. I didn't understand what she meant but didn't ask for clarification. There have always been autobiographical traits in my work. History deconstructed into small events. And I have been mesmerised by the silence of images.

I didn't open the album for almost a decade. What could I do with pages of images of a baby boy born in the spring of 1944?

>   water soluble
>   potentially explosive
>   toxic

*

In 2016, I went to Lviv in Ukraine, formerly Lwów in Poland or Lemberg in the Austro-Hungarian Empire: the contested city of my father's birth where most of the images in the album had been taken. There was no agenda for that trip. What sparked it was a benign curiosity and an almost random choice of destination. For quite some time, each late winter, in February, I have travelled somewhere I have never been before. These have always been solitary adventures taken to use up leftover holidays at the end of a financial year. Athens / Los Angeles / Lviv.

>   Not combustible but enhances combustion of other substances.
>   When heated to decomposition, emits toxic fumes of
>   nitrogen oxides.
>   Decomposes at 440 °C into metallic silver, nitrogen, oxygen
>   and nitrogen oxides.

I spent my days wandering the ancient, cobbled streets, staring at the picturesque ruination. There was a sense of time in the texture of that city: uneven / peeling / faded. Lviv's beauty was of an unpristine type. Unpolished / unmodernised / underinvested. The teeth of time were most visible on the city's famous balconies. It felt as if a breath could send them tumbling down to the crooked pavements. The city was old. The city was tired.

> Goggles or face shield; rubber gloves.
> Do not eat, drink, or smoke during work.
> Wash hands before eating.
> Prevent dispersion of dust.

I carried Lviv—or Lwów or Lemberg—back within me. It had become an obsession. A crumbling city / a lost city / a found city / a city beyond the border.

> First Aid[2]
> Ensure that medical personnel are aware of the material(s) involved and take precautions to protect them. Move victim to fresh air. Call 911 or emergency medical service. Give artificial respiration if victim is not breathing. Administer oxygen if breathing is difficult. Remove and isolate contaminated clothing and shoes. Contaminated clothing may be a fire risk when dry. In case of contact with substance, immediately flush skin or eyes with running water for at least 20 minutes. Keep victim calm and warm.

For months, I meandered Lviv' streets in memory and on Google Street View. By then, I was looking for something. There was a faint thread of a story developing. A feeling / a setting / a time / a loss. But there were no characters. And no plot.

> UN Hazard Class: 5.1[3]

*

---

[2] Excerpt from *ERG Guide 140 (Oxidizers)*, ERG, 2016
[3] ILO International Chemical Safety Cards (ICSC)

One day, I opened the album my mother had given me. I have no memory of the circumstances. Was it in winter / spring / summer? I remember flipping through the pages of images and feeling disappointed that there were no wide shots. There were no images revealing surroundings. No rooms / no views / no buildings / no city. Just people cut out from the world around them, confined to the narrow frames of the images. The photographer focused on his intimate subjects. He knew what was beyond the frame. It was his world. He didn't consider sharing it. He didn't consider that this world—his world—wouldn't last much longer.

> **Silver nitrate appears as a colourless or white crystalline solid becoming black on exposure to light or organic material.**

Flipping through the pages, back and forth, I came across the single, loose image tucked in between them. Another medium shot. A portrait. Loaded with sadness. The posture of the woman. The stillness of the child sitting next to her. Their eyes looking somewhere outside the frame. The photograph had weight.

> **All forms of silver are cumulative once they enter body's tissues, and very little is excreted.**

I kept on returning to the image. I kept on looking at the woman and the little girl. I knew this was my grandmother, who I had never met, and my aunt, my father's older sister, who had died a year or so before him. But there was something not quite right about the image. The angle. The framing. And the focus was wrong. Neither the woman's face nor the child's was sharp. As if the photograph was taken in haste. Without much concentration. Or as if someone distracted the photographer, who still pressed the shutter release to capture the moment. In an imperfect image.

> When silver ions interact with proteins, physical properties of
> the protein are usually altered.

And then, I saw what the image was about. I looked beyond the two people in the frame towards the edges. Towards the focal point. Towards the odd focal point. And it all fell into place.

> An intimate mixture of dry powdered magnesium and silver
> nitrate may ignite explosively on contact with a drop of water.

The woman and the child were framed by cargo train doors. It was 1944. Late spring. Hot. The fate of the city had already been sealed months earlier at the Tehran Conference.

> Silver nitrate reacts with acetylene in presence of ammonia to
> form silver acetylide, a sensitive and powerful detonator when dry.

*

Something had come to an end. Even if they could not have fully grasped it in that moment. There was a road ahead. A road untravelled. A road with an unknown terminus. Even if there was a destination written onto the side of the train and into their swastika-stamped travel permits. They were not being deported. Deportations came earlier and later. In different directions. They *missed* those trains. Although they could never be too sure. With all the secrets they carried.

> Interaction between silver nitrate and chlorosulfonic acid
> is violent.

*

I kept on thinking of what was beyond the frame of the image: the platform / the train station / crates / looted artworks / tanks / guns / grenades / motorcycles / trucks / hail hitler / schneller / leather / shoe polish / swastikas / flags / civilians / refugees / retreating German troops / approaching Soviets / blown-up synagogues / ash / hunger / fear / grief / traces / survival / resistance / blood / Lwów / Lemberg / soon to become Lvov, USSR / then Lviv, Ukraine / Allies' bombers in the sky / three hundred kilometres / twenty-four hours.

> A solution of silver nitrate is mixed into a warm gelatin containing potassium bromide, sodium chloride or other alkali metal halides.

The image captured the essence of leaving. A *mundane* outcome of war. They did not know how much future there was ahead.

> A reaction precipitates fine crystals of insoluble silver halides that are light sensitive.

A small wartime story. A small moment. A true moment. I held that moment in my hands. I knew it had happened. I could see the light of that moment in the image. It was there. Preserved.

> The type and quantity of gelatin used influences the final emulsion's properties.

I set out to write a story from that moment. From that frame. Expanding it in every direction, across four (or five or six) dimensions. And layering it with characters, settings and events. Creating a plausible unreality. A fabrication / a fantasy / an invention / an illusion / a reverie / a figment / a fiction. With imagination. An adhesive that was missing at the back of the image.

> A pH buffer, crystal habit modifier, metal dopants, ripener, ripening restrainer, surfactants, defoamer, emulsion stabiliser and biocide are also used in emulsion making.

*

A photograph is not a story.

> Most modern emulsions are 'washed' to remove some of the reaction by-products.

It is a frame / a moment / a 1/60th of a second (more or less).

> The washing or desalting step can be performed by ultrafiltration, dialysis, coagulation or a classic noodle washing method.

A connection to reality. A chemical connection to reality that sparks a reaction.

> Emulsion making also incorporates steps to increase sensitivity by using chemical sensitising agents and sensitising dyes.

*

A photograph is a memory within a grain of salt.

> Silver nitrate is far less sensitive to light than the halides. It was once called lunar caustic because silver was called *luna* by the ancient alchemists, who associated silver with the moon.

A grain of truth to seed a story.

GYABIDIE

D U
 A
  A

   N
   E

LABEJA KODUA OKULU

It was a harmattan night in Accra, Ghana. The salt of the sea and the sounds of Sakumono beach slowly overpowered the night and the choral voices of hawkers and traffic moved into a subtle hum. I sat awake on several straw mats, alone in an empty house that is deep in conversation with itself. On this night, however, I felt like it wanted to talk to me. I had been left alone in a family friend's house, my parents and younger sister in a much fancier place, too polite to ask for extra space for me. I gave up the chance to be served breakfast in the early mornings and settled for an old house, where the wood talks.

    I was initially frightened by the speech of the house, it seemed insistent, knocking on the door to the living room where I was sleeping, tapping along the corners of the roof, the television volume turned up to the max in order to not speak with it. However, as the night wore on, I began to listen closely, to engage with the turns and twists, and the minute dancing of the strands of the planks between brick and corrugated sheet, I was soothed in the night by my interpretation of its particular morse code. I didn't know where the wood came from, whether it was wawa or odum, oak or beech, it still held the acrid scent of turpentine. The doors had bent so the locks needed changing. A flimsy shed door bolt tacked on to an ageing frame was the only thing that protected me from the elements.

> *I was used when still carrying water / my exertion to keep to the bolts of my structure / means I have to twist towards the strictures of my being / patience disappears for those who need a home / all my being is a dance / it was harmattan / but they couldn't wait / I have a voice / I have some movement / I can turn so light shines on the sofa / and rainwater*
>
>   *leaks*
>   *through.*

I thought of all the things I could say to the wood, so forlorn, so desperate for conversation, that it would make the aluminium sheets rattle with pressure. I remember bursting with all the things I could say. I remember weeping because I couldn't speak,
I had so many jokes to give. I knew how it felt to shiver with the need for conversation, resonating everything around me with discomfort.

> *We both have sat in the Tema sun / our bodies became languid itching with the heat / to stretch further / you grew with me / you creaked and snapped, your growing pains matched mine / and now in the cool night, with the briny breeze of the sea / salving our pain / calming us to our origins / I lose part of myself every evening / why do we hold each other down / I am slowly losing all fluid within myself / I will begin to bend toward my liberation / will you join me? / or will you still hold me down / when did this become a liberation song? I only wanted to shelter—*

I felt like I should begin confessing. I wanted to not be a bother, I only wanted to insist on being a shelter to the comfort of others. I sat and shook against the straw mat on the floor, against the light duvet around my arms, against the loud television, against the solitude of the evening, and I banged the floor hoping that the wood could say something soothing to me. And a cacophony of noise passed through the room and ended at the front door, where three loud echoing bangs of the warped door rang into the room. I drifted off to sleep, thinking, nay, hoping that this was an affirmation of our shared troubles. I promised I would remember to listen to the conversation of wood—

> *So slow and worn*
> *but isn't that truth*
> *it gets old, it gets aged.*
>> *The wood talks, the wood*
>> *creaks, a holy church that*
>> *speaks in the evening*
>> *after stretching in a daylight*
>>> *yawn to the sun*
>>> *and then folding over in the*
>>> *night, asking for conversation*
>>> *before rest*

I turned my attention from then on to the wild conversations of wood, concentrating on its extended family. I listened to the groans of centenarian forests, I walked past lumber mills and raised the sweet smelling shavings closer to my face, hoping to hear a whisper. I walked past the coal-burning fields, listening to the hiss of transformation. I realised that wood never stops engaging with its family. It always opens opportunities to speak, a democracy in every incarnation. I would regularly light a coal-pot in the garden for my mother. I poured the charcoal into the pot and with no kerosene to light it, sat for a quiet moment before the coal spoke:

> *I know of one / who I want to sing with me / we both speak the language of fire / we both rise to the sky / with plumes of acrid joy / to be something other than / no wonder you believe in angels / to rise to the sky / a pillar of cloud / is a great thing / let me rise with him / I crave spiritual release / isn't the rapture joy.*

So I packed paper underneath the coals, and packed paper underneath the grate and with a match—witness this chain of salvation—I lit the paper, and when it had exhausted itself, when it had risen to the heavens with a joyful thanks to the coal, the coal began to sing and rejoice. I couldn't find a palm fan, so I took a strong piece of cardboard, this tough cousin of wood, also processed for shelter, for carrying comfort home, now a fan for the inevitable flames. As the makeshift cardboard fan blew loud whispers of encouragement, the coal blushed scarlet and it fed me with a constant heat. Shy to the point of speechlessness, it occasionally burst forth with a torrent of gratitude and sparks, and there I leave it with a pot of water and eternal grace.

Further into the future, I sit in a life drawing class, rising to pick out a pencil, I see a large cylinder of charcoal and as I place the paper on my wooden drawing board, tape it down and scratch the surface with the coal, that malleable black line whispers to me—

Thank you, thank you, thank you.

HOMES(EA)CK

FANI KOSTOUROU

I

Even if everything else stays still, you move.
Perpetually. Infinitely. Unceasingly.

Sometimes your movement is imperceptible, light
    back
                and
                              forth,
                              back
                and
    forth.

Μην ξεγελαστείς: η θάλασσα κινείται πάντα. Δε βλέπεις ποτέ τα ίδια νερά.

Other times your movement is aggressive, it comes
with force
                      and
                                      rush.

This is when you become most mesmerising. You
withdraw yourself only to come back stronger and strike
the shore that restrains you.

Escape.

«Βλέπεις τη μάνα τρικυμία σαν αρχόντισσα να συναδράχνει τα δρακόντεια παιδιά της τα γαλανόστηθα κύματα στον πόλεμο τον αναμάρτητο με τ' άστρα.»[1]

Escape.

The heavier you are, the stiller I feel.

Δε την φοβάμαι. Μοιραζόμαστε τον ίδιο πόθο. Έχουμε την ίδιο καημό.

Escape.

I realise how hopelessly placeless I've become.

«Παιδί ακόμα, εσκεπτόμουν το ρυθμό του φλοίσβου της. Ξαπλωμένος στην αμμουδιά, εταξίδευα με τα καράβια που περνούσαν. Ένας κόσμος γεννιόταν γύρω μου....»[2]

You have always stretched beyond my sight. My arms are not wide enough to grasp your profound unboundedness.

Είναι απέραντη, δεσποτική. Δε μπορείς να την δαμάσεις.

«...Οι αύρες μού άγγιζαν τα μαλλιά. Άστραφτε η μέρα στο πρόσωπό μου και στα χαλίκια. Όλα μου ήταν ευπρόσδεκτα: ο ήλιος, τα λευκά σύννεφα, η μακρινή βοή της»[3]

Έχει σώμα, βγάζει κραυγή, από τις φωνές των πλασμάτων που κατοικούνε μέσα της.

'The starfish, the horseshoe crab, the whale's backbone;
The pools where it offers to our curiosity
The more delicate algae and the sea anemone.
It tosses up our losses, the torn seine,
The shattered lobster pot, the broken oar
And the gear of foreign dead men.
The sea has many voices,
Many gods and many voices.'[4]

Για να «βρίσκει ἡ νοσταλγία μας διέξοδο καὶ ὁ πόνος μας τὴν ἔκφρασή του.»[5]

II

Nothing embraces all my senses like you.
I'm bawling. I'm dripping.
This is what I am made of.
Salt water.

Η θάλασσα φέρει κάτι από τους ανθρώπους που την διέσχισαν.
Θύμησες από προηγούμενες ζωές και περασμένους έρωτες.
Γίνεται τρύπα για τους φίθυρους αυτού του κόσμου.

«κάποτε, αν κάποιος είχε ένα μυστικό το οποίο δεν ήθελε να μοιραστεί, πήγαινε σε ένα βουνό, έβρισκε ένα δέντρο, άνοιγε μια τρύπα σε αυτό και φιθύριζε το μυστικό μέσα στην τρύπα. Στη συνέχεια το κάλυπτε με λάσπη. Και άφηνε το μυστικό για πάντα εκεί»[6]

You listen to my whispers.
I talk about foreign waters. How they caress,
how they kiss. How they seduce me and lure me at night.

Μια μάγισσα πλανεύτρα που έχει τρόπους να σου κλέβει, να σου δίνει και να σου παίρνει.

«Αλίμονο αν κόψουμε τα μπάνια μόνο και μόνο γιατί πνίγηκαν πεντέξι. Αλίμονο αν προδώσουμε τη θάλασσα γιατί έχει τρόπους να μας καταπίνει.»[7]

I mourn the waters that swallowed me.
'No man moved me till the tide, Went past my simple shoe,
And past my apron and my belt, And past my bodice too,
And made as he would eat me up As wholly as a dew'[8]

The same waters that washed me ashore.

Και κάθε τόσο παλεύεις με ξένα νερά. Ώσπου δεν σε χωράει καμιά στεριά πια.

III

'So, here you are
too foreign for home too foreign for here.
Never enough for both.'[9]

Where did I start and where do I want to go?
What land can hold me now that I have learned to swim
away your cascades?

Δεν είναι εύκολο να φεύγεις. Ούτε να μένεις είναι εύκολο βέβαια. Όταν έχεις ταξιδέψει, η θάλασσα γίνεται δρόμος κι η μόνη Ιθάκη σου.

I slowly grow roots in your ground,
To find the home I lost and will never have again.

«καὶ βλέπω τὰ ὀνείρατα κι ἀκούω τὰ μιλήματα τῶν πρώτων μου χρόνων κοντὰ στὸ ἀκρογιάλι, στενάζεις καρδιά μου τὸ ἴδιο ἀναστέναγμα: Νὰ ζοῦσα καὶ πάλι στὴ θάλασσα ἐκεῖ τὴ ρηχὴ καὶ τὴν ἥμερη, στὴ θάλασσα ἐκεῖ τὴν πλατιά, τὴ μεγάλη.» [10]

For you fill the space in-between spaces.
A home for the placeless of this world, for those who don't belong, who are transient, displaced or uninvested. For those who wander but never arrive. For those who flee and those who dream.

They carry you inside.

Attuning to your movement.
Rejoicing in your light and voice.
Washing their wounds and cooling off their bodies.
Whispering their secrets to your hole.
Tossing up their losses in your tide.

Pouring the ugliness of this world around them.
Filling and pouring.

---

1   Θάλασσα: η αρχαιότητα της γεωγραφίας, Νίκος Καρούζος
2   Το Εγκώμιο της Θαλάσσης, Κώστας Καρυωτάκης
3   Το Εγκώμιο της Θαλάσσης, Κώστας Καρυωτάκης
4   *The Dry Salvages (No. 3 of 'Four Quartets')*, T.S. Elliot
5   Το Εγκώμιο της Θαλάσσης, Κώστας Καρυωτάκης
6   *2046*, Wong Kar-wai
7   Η θάλασσα, Ντίνος Χριστιανόπουλος
8   *By the sea*, Emily Dickinson
9   *Diaspora blues*, Ijeoma Umebinyuo
10   Μια πίκρα, Κωστής Παλαμάς

THE VIEW

THWO TURPIN

Outside is the sea
And its faint aroma brings to mind images of
a future
A future where we might lie here forever.

All around us is view
An unbroken, unbreakable image waiting to be
jumped into.

In the background, I can hear the faint sound of
boats and I imagine the men going out to work
But how could you work with such beauty?
How could you do anything other than sink in and be
drunk by it?

Just like at E10-27,
I too could go out into the waves and never
come back
Be found washed up on the beach next day.
I, the old man, the creator
After a life of taming, I could not match you
Your strength, your colour, your relentlessness,
your truth.
You inspire and you humble.
But where are you going now?
As the sky darkens and the flickering light from
the central stone fireplace sparks a reflection
which blocks you from me.
Each time I am struck dumb again
Lustful and jealous
Like a teenager left alone at the bus stop,
watching as you leave

Unable to express how much I hurt, it is too real.
You.
Only you.

As my eyes scan the horizon, the great horizontal,
my nose gently presses the cold of the window
pane
And I wonder whether you do it, daily, just to play
with me, as if to keep me hooked.
But, my love, you don't have to, I am already
jealous, already deeply drawn.

It is the presence of you, the other, who, with all
of your complexity, may both light up and
drown me in dark.
I, with this feeling of heartbreak, swore that I would
grow and would build a frame for you
Not to tame you, who could wish to do such a
thing? Just to explain you
To me.

I have designed something special for you
Although traditionally rectangular in shape my ode
contains five glazed panes
Each spirals out from the centre in homage to your perfect
                                                              geometries.
Mine is made of oak and sat within a casement
of lumpen rock
Yours contains everything and nothing at all.

But why do you always go?
I will have to watch videos of you until again
you show.

Separation is the hardest thing,

The view through my window
The view through my phone
The view through my screen
The view through my mind
The view through my psyche
The view is me.

https://open.spotify.com/playlist/3frReYxwJeaeRushzG3Cr5

COLLECTIVE DISPLAY OF AFFECTION

Lea Collet, Miriam Austin, Harry Bix, Geundalina Cerruti, Rosa Doornenbal, Rotman Gatk, Maria Gorodeckaya, Natalia Janula, Eleni Papazoglou, Anna Souter, Zaiba Jabbar, Lou-Atessa Marcellin, Naz Balkaya, Dylan Spencer-Davidson

We are naked at birth
Conscious of who we are
and we cannot renounce the name 'human'.
If our definition (human) is false,
then we shall die.
If our definition (human) is right,
then we should keep it and transmit it
and
we shall live.

        I transcend my positivity
            I surrender myself to the sun

Does anyone know how to build something?
Maybe we could build a plane?
Or someone could send a car to get us?
To go where though?

A double pop

popping illusions

I wonder

a party?

Old fashion,
my heart is racing like the first day of school.
I'm a stranger in this town.

    I transcend my positivity
        I surrender myself to the sun

Through an apparent retrograde motion
the chemical started to penetrate me.
It first started in my head,
went through my fingers,
down to my feet
and is now going into the ground.

      I transcend my positivity
         I surrender myself to the sun

Illness came with no surprise.
Everything seems to be broken;
The chain
Your body
The left speaker
Our link
The placing of things makes more sense now.
I transcend my positivity
I surrender myself to the sun
and
landed on the island.

I keep getting closer to you
                              I keep

                              I keep

                              I keep

                                          I keep missing you.

you get your diagnosis on the day i land.
me in my old childhood room,
you, in your hospital bed across town.
we exchange links on politics and race and transgender rights,
my iphone to your burner phone.
the kinds of conversations we'd never been able to have.

i'm coming down after a week of romance,
high peak of emotion,
love in the summer in paris.

                                                            now,
                            none of the places feel right.

my therapist says don't focus on the relationship,
focus on the doubts.
and as i hang up,
i light the cigarette and empty the ashtray for the second time today.

                          I transcend my positivity
                                      I surrender myself to the sun

when you're drunk you're terrific,
when you're drunk I like you mostly
late at night, you're quite alright.
But I can't understand the different you
in the morning when it's time to play
at being human for a while.
Please smile.[1]

[1] Robert Wyatt, *Sea Song.*

https://vimeo.com/686222764

NOTES ON LETTERS

BLUE, BLUE, BRILLIANT BLUE
Carolina Ramirez-Figueroa

The genus Paenibacillus are rod-shaped gram-positive or gram-variable, endospore-forming bacteria which have been isolated from a variety of sources including soil, fresh and saltwater, sewage, sediments, caves, humus, compost, rhizosphere, food, plants, insect larvae and clinical samples. Paenibacillus are bacterial species that secretes lubricant chemicals, and possess a flagellum which enables them to slide easily on hard surfaces. Paenibacillus species are also distinctive for their colony cooperation and signalling behaviours. The T morphotype, for example, gets its name from a tendency for tip-splitting while the C, short for chirality, develops branches that grow into a twisting pattern. A different morphotype, V (vortex), is characterised by tip vortices, which are linked to the clustering of hundreds of millions of cells that circle around a common centre, a behaviour which enables colonies to organise in cooperative tasks.

Paenibacillus and I go back a long way. I first met them through a series of pictures taken by Dr Ben Jacob, whose research group are credited with isolating and classifying the species. I wrote to him and he generously sent me samples of the vortex, T and C morphotypes which I used during my PhD as I was exploring bacterial patterning and different ways of 'controlling' their morphologies. Paenibacillus are particularly hard to grow — they duplicate quickly and grow as a transparent film on hard media. The one way to 'visualise' them is to stain them with Brilliant Blue R staining solution commonly used in microbiology.

Staining them binds a colouring agent to specific proteins present in the bacteria, with the caveat that this kills the organism in the process.

(FRAILEJÓN)
Mónica Rivas Velásquez

The film *(frailejón)* is an extract from my research on and with the Páramos and Frailejones, *More than an Object, its Shadow*.

Páramos are high altitude forests of the tropical Andes, of which Colombia has the largest number. They are complex ecosystems, key due to their immense biodiversity. They are almost impossible to define in a short paragraph, but surely necessary to recall when thinking of affective exchanges with other-than-humans.

Páramos host more than 4,000 vegetable species, one of which is frailejón, also known as Espeletia. Similar to other Páramo plants, frailejones have the ability to absorb water from fogs and rains through an adaptation of their leaves, in order to funnel it into streams and contribute water storage back into the soil. Colombian páramos supply over 70% of the water for the population.

Páramos are mysterious, sacred and longed for. They are also exploited and are currently under severe threat from several factors, including large-scale mining and climate change. A thorough regulation (Ley, 1930) has been recently put in place to redefine their boundaries and restrict harmful activities. This law, which seeks to support their sustainability, is not free of challenges. At present, a significant effort is being made to work with páramos inhabitants, unpacking their own understanding of the law itself and their approach to its eventual implementation.

Thinking about land and territory means thinking and collaborating with the people who inhabit it.

SUPERCRITICAL, A PSALM
Adam Moore

Supercritical, a Psalm, is a love affair between interior and exterior bodies of water. Pivotal to Moore's practice is the synthesis of embodied knowledge with transdisciplinary practice for more artful/skilful living. For *Supercritical, a Psalm*, Moore draws on his embodied encounters with different modes of locomotion used to inhabit and navigate local bodies of water in Newham, East London, where he was born, grew up, and lives today. Observing, sensing, and moving within the architectural, elemental, social, and spatial relations around the docklands, Moore investigates this unique cityscape and its riverways on the peripheries of the city, from the Royal Victoria Docks to Royal Albert Wharf and beyond. *Supercritical, a Psalm*, engages with these inspiring urban waterscapes through nature writing, moving image, and Moore's archive of embodied encounters within this fluid and developing site of regeneration.

THE PARIS FOLLIES
Himali Singh Soin

At the Georgia Fee Writers Residency in Paris, Himali Singh Soin utilised the romantic clichés of Paris to excavate its less probable, scientific desires. From 18th century follies in Parc Monceau and Bois de Vincennes, to 20th century follies in Le Parc de la Villette, to modern buildings like La Grande Arche to Gargoyles, and mere street side ornaments, her lines were made of hypercubes, topologies, tangles and tautologies. When Haussmann planned Paris, center quadrants giving way to five radiating boulevards, he did not foresee that it would be a city full of stars, lingering long after their time. In Paris, city of light, the particle swerves into the wave, sine-like and full of signifiers. In Paris, city of love, Himali speculates on whether its most magical romance might be found in its most foolish mathematics.

MARSEILLE CANAL
John Bingham-Hall

Following an era of drought, disease, and accompanying social unrest in the 'Phocean city', the Canal de Marseille was built in stages between 1838 and 1881, channeling water from the Durance river further north to irrigate and hydrate Marseille and its region, via 200 kilometres of tunnel and aqueduct. Transforming the rocky hinterland into fertile agricultural terrain, it tripled the city's inhabitants and until the 1970s, remained one of its few sources of drinking water. Known by its landmarks (the Pavillon de partage des eaux des Chutes-Lavie; the Palais Longchamp; or the Aqueduc de Roquefavour) the majority of the canal itself is hidden underground or (formally) inaccessible behind barriers, even though it still provides nearly two thirds of Marseille's water. I followed its route as closely as possible for 10 kilometres from Saint-Antoine in the northern quarters of Marseille, reuniting with it wherever I could, and telling it my thoughts. This love letter is a reminder to myself to think of the canal and its long journey every time I drink a glass of water.

LUNAR CAUSTIC: A MEMORY WITHIN A GRAIN OF SALT
Marta Michalowska

Lunar Caustic: A Memory within a Grain of Salt collects reflections on photography and fiction, first drafted in late 2021, sparked by the process of writing *Sketching in Ashes*, a novel about violence and its typology and topology, about looking far not to look close, and the tension between fleeing and standing one's ground, set across London (UK), Sopot (Poland), Lviv (Ukraine) and the borderlands between Poland, Ukraine and Belarus. They have a different resonance now. A chilling resonance. With air raid shelters / bombed train stations / looted artworks / tanks / flags / civilians / refugees / fear / grief / survival / resistance as the European reality in the present rather than in the past.

It is dedicated to all those forced to leave their homes who do not know when / if they will be able to return.

DUA NE GYABIDIE
Labeja Kodua Okullu

... touch wood.
    carve your name on the bark.
We imbue power into wood, we use it daily in all its iterations, from the calm respite under an oak's leaves, to the heat of a charcoal burner, all the way down to the daily scratchings and musings on paper, cardboard and poster. It follows us, calmly, providing support, providing warmth, providing a space for our history.

HOMES(EA)CK
Fani Kostourou

Homes(ea)ck is a multi-voiced song of praise to and for the sea written in English and Greek. Different addresses, to the sea, the reader, or oneself, entangle with passages from works of poetry and are lined up in different columns. Narrative cartographies of sensations, bodies and contextual forces follow them.

THE VIEW
Theo Turpin

When asked to write a love letter to the 'more than human' I couldn't shake the idea that I could only view this concept/entity/relationship through my own very human gaze. Therefore, I decided that I would do what humans do and set out to frame this idea. But what is the 'more than human' to me? It is clearly something non-homosapien, probably with a complex set of relationships with other entities which surround it, but again I can only view it as me, I can only view it through an emotive gaze. Then I realised that it is exactly this 'view' that is 'more than human', it is the emotional response to a system which I gaze upon, a system which is vastly older and more complex than I. One which I, and my kind, have built portals to frame and reproduced likenesses in dedication to, one which we have twisted and mutated to fit our desires. This, therefore, is my love letter to 'the view'.

COLLECTIVE DISPLAY OF AFFECTION

Lea Collet, Miriam Austin, Harry Bix, Guendalina Cerruti, Rosa Doornenbal, Roxman Gatt, Maria Gorodeckaya, Natalia Januła, Eleni Papazoglou, Anna Souter, Zaiba Jabbar, Lou-Atessa Marcellin, Naz Balkaya, Dylan Spencer-Davidson

I recall intimacies that I share, challenge, and negate with others, intimacies that allow new and alternative stories to be told. In this process, I explore the importance of collective affection and how it can organise our beings. The enormous power of symbiosis seems more urgent than ever. Let's go back to the cells, to the ability of different organisms to live together and share roles. The etymology of symbiosis literally means 'living' and 'together'. —Lea Collet

BIOGRAPHIES

DR. JOHN BINGHAM-HALL

Dr. John Bingham-Hall is European project Associate for Theatrum Mundi Europe. He is interested in in performances, infrastructures, and technologies of shared life in the city. With a background in music (Goldsmiths) and architectural theory (UCL Bartlett), he works across artistic, spatial and critical humanities to question and participate in the making of the urban public sphere. Since 2015, he has initiated projects with Theatrum Mundi on cultural infrastructure, urban commons, political voice, and sonic urbanism. Alongside this he has collaborated on research projects at LSE and Oxford; taught at CSM and UCL; published writing across scholarly and arts platforms; and organised queer cultural events (serving drinks whenever needed).

ANDREA CETRULO

Andrea Cetrulo is a curator, sociologist and DJ, and has an affinity for architecture, philosophy, the Atlantic Ocean, and wine. She studied Sociology at the University of Barcelona, and Urban Studies at University College London. She shares her life-long fascination with the occult through her monthly show on Noods, a UK independent radio station.

COLLECTIVE DISPLAY OF AFFECTION

Collective Display of Affection is a sharing of ideas on collective affection, ecology, technology and agency as explored by a group of creative practitioners who gathered through the Camden Art Center Peer Forum 2020 programme in partnership with Artquest. The group led by artist Lea Collet includes Miriam Austin, Harry Bix, Guendalina Cerruti Rosa Doornenbal, Roxman Gatt, Maria Gorodeckaya, Natalia Januła, Eleni Papazoglou Anna Souter, Zaiba Jabbar, Lou-Atessa Marcellin, Naz Balkaya, Dylan Spencer-Davidson.

LABEJA KODUA OKULLU

Labeja is a Ghanaian-British writer who lives in London. After studying English and Comparative Literature at Goldsmiths, he went on to complete The Novel Studio writing course at City, University of London and is currently working on his first novel. Labeja has published poetry with *Forward Poetry* and *Rattle* magazine and has essays with *The Smart Set* magazine and has contributed a poem to *Interior Realms* published by Theatrum Mundi.

FANI KOSTOUROU

Fani Kostourou is an architect and urbanist, holding a PhD from UCL Bartlett. She is Urban Computation Specialist at Grimshaw Architects and an Associate Lecturer at the University for the Creative Arts and Central Saint Martins. Fani works with curatorial and editorial projects, exhibiting and publishing internationally on spatial design and theories, housing, morphology and urban cultures. Some of her most recent works include *Do you hear Athens?* a 24-hour audio piece exploring the Athenian balcony as a threshold space between domestic and public spheres, and Movement Forum a mobile laboratory exploring the design of urban (im)mobilities in Lisbon, London and Paris. Fani has a soft spot for the sea, finding comfort in what she calls home.

MARTA MICHALOWSKA

Marta Michalowska is a curator, artist and writer based in London. She has recently completed her debut novel *Sketching in Ashes*, supported by Arts Council England through the Developing Your Creative Practice programme, and is currently writing her second, *A Tram to the Beach*; both novels explore contested territories. She graduated from the Novel Studio at City, University of London, in 2019. Her short stories were published by *Migrant Journal* and *Litro*, as well as in collections *Interior Realms* and *Concrete and Ink: Storytelling and the Future of Architecture*. Marta is Director of the Wapping Project.

ADAM MOORE

Adam Moore is a British-St. Lucian artist from East London. His work explores themes of multiculturalism, unity and resilience at the intersectional discourses and embodied explorations of sustainability. A transdisciplinary artist who dances and works with dance, his work with diverse groups across human rights, non-profit arts and culture, and social wellbeing informs his approach to sustainability, collaboration and art making. He teaches on the Contemporary Performance Practice: Experimental Arts and Performance programme at the Royal Central School of Speech and Drama, and co-designs and facilitates Camden Art Centre's Youth Collective *Transformative Futures* programme.

DR. CAROLINA RAMIREZ-FIGUEROA

Carolina Ramirez-Figueroa is a Research Tutor in Design Products at the Royal College of Art, where she leads the Design Futures Pathway, and a theory tutor at the Masters in Architectural Design at the Bartlett, School of Architecture at UCL. Her research explores the challenges and opportunities found when living systems are understood as matter. She is interested in exploring the cultures, practices, tools and economies of working and designing with living systems. Her PhD thesis, *Bio-material probes: design engagements with living systems*, proposed a creative exploration methodology based on direct engagements that helps to articulate a sense of ethics of care across species. Carolina has collaborated with a number of artists, designers and scientists, and exhibited in different art and design venues around the world including Helsinki, Edinburgh, Belgium, Canada, Taiwan and Japan, and more recently at the Barbican Centre as part of the exhibition Biological Buildings, and at Sheffield at the Festival of the Mind.

MÓNICA RIVAS VELÁSQUEZ

Mónica Rivas Velásquez is a Colombian artist living in London, working with expanded notions of drawing, embodied narratives and the coming together of image, text and voice. Her most recent project, currently developed in her AHRC funded PhD, *More Than an Object, its Shadow**, interrogates ways of learning through encounters with Colombian plants (*frailejones*) belonging to the ecosystem *el páramo*; high altitude Andean forests, key in the production and storage of water for most of the country. *MOS* manifests iteratively as collages and drawings, publications, performative readings, lectures, and sound works. It has been staged at ICA, Stanley Picker Gallery, South London Botanical Institute, AWL Radio, Theatrum Mundi, Clouds and Tracks, Radiophrenia, Café Oto and Fieldnotes Audio. * (Title borrowed from the Brazilian author Clarice Lispector's novel *Água Viva*)

space. Between 2012 and 2013, he was artist in residence at Palais De Tokyo, Paris, where he realised numerous works including a solo presentation. Between 2015 and 2016, Theo undertook residencies at The Embassy of Foreign Artists, Ministry for culture, Geneva as well as taking part in the summer school of the ICA Moscow. He has exhibited widely at Palais De Tokyo, Manifesta 13, the Biennale D'Anglet, The Forgotten Bar in Berlin and DKUK, Auto Italia, Tenderpixel and Bold Tendencies in London, among others. His work can be found in magazines and publications such as *Beaux Arts*, *Palais* and *Twin* and he has just published his first book entitled *Into the Night*, a collection of short stories published by Atlas Projectos. He is currently a Doctoral researcher at Loughborough University.

HIMALI SINGH SOIN

Himali is a writer and artist based between London and Delhi. She uses metaphors from outer space and the natural environment to construct imaginary cosmologies of interferences, entanglements, deep voids, debris, delays, alienation, distance and intimacy. In doing this, she thinks through ecological loss, and the loss of home, seeking shelter somewhere in the radicality of love. Her speculations are performed in audio-visual, immersive environments.

THEO TURPIN

Theo Turpin is an artist producing installations which explore how language, narrative and romance combine to make ideal and idealised

A LOVE AFFAIR

Editorial and Concept
  Lou-Atessa Marcellin

Text
  Carolina Ramirez-Figueroa, Mónica Rivas Velásquez, Adam Moore, Andrea Cetrulo, Himali Singh Soin, John Bingham-Hall, Marta Michalowska, Labeja Kodua Okullu, Fani Kostourou, Theo Turpin, Collective Display of Affection

Proofreading
  Imogen Free

Design
  ATLAS Projectos

Typefaces
  Victor, **Vremena Grotesk**, Baskerville, **TURPIN**

Printing
  Grafiche Veneziane – Società Cooperativa, Venice

This work is subject to copyright. All rights reserved. No part of this publication may be reproduced, translated, stored in a retrieval system, or transmitted in any form or by any means, electronic or mechanical, without prior written permission from Theatrum Mundi.

Copyright ©Theatrum Mundi, 2023

Image credits
  All images © Theo Turpin, 2023.

ISBN : 978-1-3999-4018-4

Published by Theatrum Mundi
  in partnership with ATLAS A.d.A.

Theatrum Mundi
c/o Groupwork
15a Clerkenwell Close
EC1R 0AA
London, UK

Theatrum Mundi Europe
59 Rue du Département
75018
Paris, France

www.theatrum-mundi.org

This publication is part of Theatrum Mundi Editions, a quarterly series reflecting current streams and new directions in our research, led by our team and collaborators, and shared with our members. Editions are generously supported by the Friends of Theatrum Mundi, who are listed in the acknowledgments. Every effort has been made to trace copyright holders and obtain their permission for the uses of copyright material. The publisher apologises for any errors and omissions and would be grateful to be notified of any corrections that should be incorporated in the future editions of this book. The right of Name of the Author to be identified as the author of this work has been asserted in accordance with Section 77 of the Copyright, Design and Patents Act 1988.

Friends of Theatrum Mundi (see https://theatrum-mundi.org/membership/)
MA Cities, Central Saint Martins
David Chipperfield Architects
Joao Villas
Nick Tyler (Patron)